LEARN2LEAD

Learn2Lead
© FIEC / The Good Book Company Ltd, 2007

The Good Book Company
Elm House, 37 Elm Road, New Malden, Surrey KT3 3HB, UK
Tel: 0845-225-0880
Fax: 0845-225-0990
Email: admin@thegoodbook.co.uk
Internet: www.thegoodbook.co.uk

ISBN 13: 978 1905564743

Printed in India

LEARN2LEAD

LEADERSHIP IN PRACTICE 2

WELCOME

Welcome to the Leadership in Practice 2 track of the *Learn2Lead* course – part of the local-church leadership training programme developed by the Fellowship of Independent Evangelical Churches. We hope you find this course both enjoyable and useful to your life and ministry.

It is likely that you will be using this book as part of a group within your congregation. But it is also possible to work through this material alone. Whichever method applies to you, we would encourage you to work prayerfully and diligently through the material, taking every opportunity to discuss the work with Christians around you.

CONTENTS

TRACK 5

LEADERSHIP IN PRACTICE 2

PREFACE

'THE THINGS YOU HAVE HEARD me say in the presence of many witnesses entrust to reliable men who will also be qualified to teach others' (2 Timothy 2:2)

Developing leaders in the church is the purpose of *Learn2Lead*. Leadership of the body of Christ is important, and therefore taking time to develop the leaders of the future is a vital aspect of building up God's church.

LEADERSHIP IS THE KEY

If you asked your Christian friends to sum up their feelings about contemporary church life, two of the words that would crop up most frequently might well be *frustration* and *disappointment*. How can that be? It's not because there's anything wrong with the gospel. That is still the power of God for the salvation of everyone who believes in the Lord Jesus Christ. It may be something to do with the way we do church. God has given us all the resources we need to fulfil his plans for this generation, but there is a crying need to discover, nurture, train and liberate the ministries of people within the church. And that means competent and effective leadership.

CHANGING THE CULTURE

Many of us come from a background where everyone expected the Minister to do everything – except perhaps play the organ, teach Sunday School or make the tea. And more disturbingly, the Minister expected it to be that way too. The vision for *Learn2Lead* is to create a culture where everyone in the church – especially young people – see leadership as something they aspire to. When Paul wrote to Timothy, he obviously expected that there would be people in the church who wanted to be leaders. We want people in the church to see their leaders at work and say, 'Under God, I'd love to be able to do that!'

WHAT IS LEARN2LEAD?

Learn2Lead is an introductory course for church members who are not in a position to take time off work for more preparation for their role as leaders. It draws on the experience of the team that already trains people through a residential and placement programme called *Prepared for Service*. When you have completed *Learn2Lead* you may consider further study under the *Prepared for Service* programme or alternatively, with the Open Bible Institute. Details of these organisations can be found at the end of this workbook.

WHO TEACHES LEARN2LEAD?

The Scriptures indicate that those who are already doing important work in the church have it as their responsibility to train others to carry forward the work. The apostle Paul told his son in the faith, Timothy, 'The things you have heard me say in the presence of many witnesses entrust to reliable men who will also be qualified to teach others' (2 Timothy 2:2).

Learn2Lead is a tool for experienced leaders to use to teach others. It is designed to help those 'at the helm' to assist a new generation of leaders as they learn how to lead others. Tutors will normally be church leaders and others whose ministry has earned the respect and confidence of those they lead.

WHO MARKS LEARN2LEAD?

Learn2Lead is a course designed for use within your congregation under the guidance of your church leader. Their feedback is going to be the most beneficial to you as they know you as a person and see your ministry in action. However, you may also like an independent person to look at your work, mark it and (if successful) issue you with a certificate that acknowledges your many hours of study. If this is the case then you are welcome to submit a folder of your work (containing answers to each of the exercises in this book) to the Open Bible Institute. For full details (including the current marking fee) please see the website: *www.open-bible-institute.org.*

WHO IS LEARN2LEAD FOR?

It is for everyone in the local church who has the potential to be a leader. And the definition of leadership? That quality that makes other people want to follow you. You may be in leadership already as an elder or youth work co-ordinator. Perhaps people in the church have suggested that you have the leadership gifts that could be developed for the future. *Learn2Lead* is not just for potential church leaders, it is also hoped that it will assist any church member who is given responsibility in the church.

FIVE TRACKS

Learn2Lead consists of five tracks of training looking at the knowledge, skills and attitudes required to be developed by leaders in the church.

Understanding the Bible, Understanding Doctrine, Understanding Leadership, Leadership in Practice 1 and Leadership in Practice 2

THREE ELEMENTS TO THE COURSE

There are three elements to the course:

1. **Individual study** – this should be done before meeting with your tutor and the group.
2. **Group session** – this would normally include a review of individual study; discussion of some of the answers; review of any action points from the previous group session and preview of the next unit to be studied etc.
3. **Ministry opportunity** – there may be ways in which the study material from the unit can be implemented in your own ministry.

So *Learn2Lead* is not just about gathering information and getting the answers right but also applying that information so that you learn by experience in the church.

THE TOOLS YOU WILL NEED

• **Bible** – *Learn2Lead* uses the NIV Bible throughout.

• **Notebook –** You will need to make a record of your answers to questions and other notes and we suggest you have a notebook which you can use in conjunction with this student manual. At the end of these ten units, there is the option to submit the work you have done for marking by the Open Bible Institute. All students who submit work of an appropriate standard will be issued with a certificate. If you would like to work towards this certificate, please keep all your answers to the unit questions in your notebook. Once you have finished unit 10, neat versions of your answers can be submitted to the Open Bible Institute with the appropriate marking fee.

• **Bible Dictionary –** It would be useful for you to have access to a good Bible Dictionary. Student discounts are available through the Open Bible Institute office.

- The Bible passages by this symbol must be read. There are also a number of other references which should be looked at if you have time.

- These questions are designed to be worked through on your own and usually have factual answers.

- These questions are designed for discussion during your group meeting. Come prepared with some ideas.

- The six Old Testament units from Understanding the Bible have questions with this symbol. They are important as they show the 'big picture' of what God planned and did through Jesus Christ throughout history.

- These are points of application and further work which will help you to develop what you have learned in the unit.

The value of *Learn2Lead* is not only found in the quality of the material but particularly in its application. This is the secret of effective leadership in the body of Christ. The *Learn2Lead* team are interested in ensuring that the words contained within this book come alive in your role of leadership and in the church as a whole. If you can help us develop the material to ensure that this continues to happen please contact us, we would love to hear how you are progressing.

Remember leadership is action – never just a position!

Learn2Lead c/o The Good Book Company,
Elm House, 37 Elm Road, New Malden, Surrey KT3 3HB
For further information please also see the FIEC website: www.fiec.org.uk

SETTING A VISION

CHILDREN AND YOUNG PEOPLE are of huge significance, aren't they? But do you realise just how big the task is of reaching them? More than 60% of the earth's six billion inhabitants are aged under 24.

What about where you live? Try to get a feel for the challenge ahead of you. Do a quick piece of homework...
1. *Find out how many youngsters attend Lower/Infants, Middle/Junior, Upper/Secondary schools near you.*
2. *Ask yourself, how many of them hear clear presentations of the gospel?*

It seems that we are not doing very well in our attempts to reach them. A recent survey of more than 700 children found that only two knew that the Millennium had anything to do with Jesus! But the Bible can help us to overcome our sense of inadequacy – it sets us a vision!

THE CHILDREN YOU CAN REACH

To get the help we need, the best place to start is with the Scriptures themselves, and where better than an example of the Apostle Paul bringing a church back to its Christian senses.

Read 1 Corinthians 9:19-23

PRINCIPLES TO BEAR IN MIND

STRATEGIES TO REACH CHILDREN

Look at verse 22.

What is Paul's goal?

How will that purpose impact upon your church schedules as you plan ahead?

There are differences of opinion and practice between those Christians who see the new covenant relating to believers only, and those who see it as including believers and their children.

Do you think of children as basically 'lost' and needing to be saved, or basically 'found' until they prove otherwise?

IDENTIFYING WITH CHILDREN

Paul bends over backwards to identify with his hearers – see verse 20.

1. *What does this imply for work with youngsters?*
2. *What barriers do we have to overcome in reaching them?*

COMMUNICATING WITH CHILDREN

Paul does all for the sake of the gospel – his goal is to win people by the gospel (v 23). That gospel must not be compromised, but...

1. *In what ways can it be adapted and still passed on faithfully to different people?*
2. *What lessons do we learn from passages like Acts 13:26-33, 14:15-18 and 17:22-31?*
3. *What can we do that will help children and young people to understand?*

SERVING CHILDREN

To win people, Paul is willing to become a 'slave' – he is at their disposal. Verse 22 also points to the huge energy investment involved in the task.

What do these verses mean for your church's approach to child outreach?

In today's world we need to be very sensitive to a raft of issues raised by the problems of child abuse. Here are two vital questions you need to consider now...

1. *Has your fellowship thought this through?*
2. *Do you have some kind of child protection policy?*

PRACTICE TO AIM FOR

Given all this 'principled pragmatism', we have received a mandate which allows great freedom, combined with a great expenditure of energy (God's energy through us – 1 Corinthians 15:10).

Given the necessity of outreach, discuss your own practice...
1. *Some Christians feel Sunday schools are a must – do you agree?*
2. *What are the alternatives?*
3. *How do you balance opportunity with resources – and with other outreach responsibilities (such as to the elderly)?*

As Paul continues in 1 Corinthians 9, he urges us to aim for 'simply the best'. We have freedom to go for...
- the best time for them
- the best place – given what you want to achieve
- the best gifts that you can muster
- the best approach for the age group with which you are working.

Rather than acting as a blueprint for children's and youth work, the Bible fires up our passion for people, encourages us to think of ways of communicating the gospel appropriately and helps us to look to the Lord for his blessing.

What is your church doing to reach youngsters with the gospel? Is it the best? Could you do what you are doing better?

THE CHURCH YOU WANT THEM TO BELONG TO

As you think about introducing children and young people to your church, it is easy immediately to think of the church we belong to, with all its foibles, rather than the church as God wants it to be. So let's start by building up from first principles, and looking at a New Testament passage…

 Read Ephesians 6:1-4

Again we will develop some key principles and begin to fill in the picture to see where the newly converted child or young person fits in.

WHAT IS RIGHT?

PARENTS' RESPONSIBILITIES

 What lessons do you learn from the following Bible passages?
- *Deuteronomy 6:1-7, 20*
- *Proverbs 1:8ff*
- *Ephesians 6:4*
- *Colossians 3:20*
- *2 Timothy 3:16*

Christian parents have the responsibility and privilege of teaching the Christian faith to their own children. Converted children with Christian parents should receive their main spiritual support from home.

 How might this happen in practice?

CHURCH RESPONSIBILITIES

 What lessons do you learn from the following Bible passages?
- *Nehemiah 8:2-3 and 8*
- *2 Chronicles 20:13*
- *Ephesians 6:1*

The Bible assumes that where parents are learning and worshipping, children will be present too. Paul addresses the children in Ephesians 6:1 assuming that they will be there.

 What about us? Do we tend to assume that children are generally incapable of listening to 'sermons' and thus remove them? Here are some tricky subjects to discuss…
- *Are our reasons for this always for the young person's benefit, or is it more to do*

with the convenience of the parents?
- *What benefits may come from keeping most of them in for the whole meeting?*
- *What problems may arise if you do this?*
- *And if you don't?*

Read Matthew 18:5-6

Christian children should be encouraged to be full and active members of the church, and should be encouraged to see the church as the primary organisation to which they are spiritually committed.

1. How can we develop this in ways appropriate to their age?
2. Discuss the role young Christians currently play in the life of your church.

We have seen that Paul does address them as a particular group needing a certain kind of teaching and advice. There is real scope for helping the young, and the growing adult. But we must make sure that we do not do this at the expense of the principles outlined above, thereby threatening the unity of the whole church. Depending on the size of the group and church, the work could well require specialist personnel (a mature woman acting as a counsellor for teenage girls, for example). There are also lots of opportunities for young people to bring the gospel to their peers in ways appropriate to their own culture.

WHAT IS WISE?

HELPING PARENTS

1. How can the church encourage Christian parents to carry out their responsibilities? Think of at least three ways.
2. Has your fellowship got anything like this in place?

HELPING CHILDREN

We need to help them by being sensitive to their different 'growth' phases. When they are very young, or are active toddlers and cannot really take part, we may spend much of our time trying slowly to train them to take part at their own level. A good crèche and other facilities will be needed for them, and for visitors' children (especially non-Christian visitors). But as they learn to sit (often by school age they are having to sit quietly) our emphasis can become one of encouraging their presence, and active participation. They will need help, but most people who take part in this phase of a child's life are amazed just how much a child can learn with even a little bit of encouragement.

We also need to be aware of the crucial importance of building good relationships. Children may relate to a few Sunday School teachers or club leaders, but the practice of quickly removing them from the meeting means that many of them rarely build relationships outside a relatively small peer group. No wonder that many don't identify with the 'adult church' as they grow and always seem to want the security of their own small circle. If that 'circle' happens to stop wanting to go to church, then the whole group can be lost to the gospel.

Discuss ways...
- *of trying to overcome this problem*
- *in which your church can support Christian children from non-Christian homes.*

Finally, we need to recall that in its care for the young, the church needs to set a standard of confidence and security for those who entrust their youngsters to its care.

HELPING THE CHURCH

The church should welcome children and help to develop lasting relationships. Some adults regularly miss the main meetings because they are caring for even quite old children. In a culture where many adults attend Sunday worship only once, this can have a detrimental effect on the life of the church. Others grow used to the absence of the children, and when they are in attendance on special occasions, there can develop a *'we suffer the little children – but only just'* mentality.

We need to encourage a loving acceptance by older members of the young, so that when they are converted they will feel part of the church, and **even if they do not become believers** they will know that the church is made up of people who really care for them – people to whom they may turn in times of crisis in later life. All this is part of the outworking of the principle of welcoming all who come.

How can you help children feel that they belong in your church?

THINK IT THROUGH

1. Can you think of action which you and your church could take to translate your 'dream' or 'vision' into practice?

2. Which do you think you are – strong on principles but weak on application? Or great on activity but not always informed by biblical principles? What steps can you take to get the balance right?

FOLLOW IT UP

1. Either formulate a 'quality review' process so that you and other leaders can sit down and ask honest questions about what you are doing with the aim of improving the overall life of the church, under the grace of God.

2. Or formulate ways in which you can help children, parents and church members to reach and integrate children and young people.

CHILDREN'S AND YOUTH WORK

TURNING VISION INTO REALITY

HAVING GRASPED the vision for reaching out to young people, how do we go about it? In this Unit, the focus is on working with young people outside our own church families, who may appear to have the greater need. In reality, however, our aim should be the same, whatever background young people are from. We want to provide for all of them:

- activities which are safe, wholesome, fun and good value for money (Ecclesiastes 11:7–12:1)
- Bible teaching which communicates clearly at their level and in their culture (1 Corinthians 9:19–23)
- role models who are examples of Christian living (2 Kings 11:21–12:2)
- the challenge of the gospel, praying that God will bring them to faith in Christ (2 Timothy 1:5).

Our overall aim is that these young people should grow up to be men and women of God, living and declaring the gospel message in their generation, as we do in ours.

WHO WILL LEAD AND WHO WILL BE INVOLVED?

Who in the church is best placed to work with young people? Older young people? Young Christians? Parents? Pastors? Deacons? Often the answer is simply whoever is willing and available. But this is an inadequate answer. Working with children is no less important to the kingdom of God than the regular preaching ministry or the proper handling of church finances. The same principles should apply to children's work as to other church work…

- What gifts are required?
- What character is needed?
- What special skills or attitudes are essential for this particular work?

1. What qualities are needed for working with children?
2. What additional gifts are required to work with teenagers?

A tall order? Perhaps. But if you substitute the word 'people' for children, you'll see that many of these gifts are required of all of us as we seek to reach out to those around us. Children are simply one special group of human beings – and in many respects are no different from others. However, there will be a demand for some special skills, and we may need some of our spiritually strongest and most gifted members to be involved in this work, not simply those who are willing to squeeze it in on top of everything else.

WHO WILL LEAD?

Whatever the size of the work in terms of numbers of children and leaders, it is best for the co-ordinator of the work not to be burdened with too many other church responsibilities. If this is not possible to start with, it should at least be an aim to work towards.

This means that it is unlikely to be best for an elder or deacon to be the overall co-ordinator (but see what is said below about accountability). If this requires some radical re-thinking of other jobs in the church, so be it!

Each separate age group or activity will need someone in charge, but the whole youth work in the church needs careful strategic thinking, planning and organisation. The co-ordinator will need to be someone respected by the other workers but also by the church leaders and the whole membership. This will be an important matter for prayer.

WHAT OTHER RESOURCES ARE NEEDED?

This cannot be an exhaustive list, but the following seem essential if the work is to be successful.

Things to have:

- Premises – church owned or rented? suitability, availability, cost?
- Insurance – public liability, equipment
- Safety procedures – first aid, accident and evacuation procedures
- Child Protection Policy for the protection of workers and children
- Games equipment and suitable storage space
- Craft materials – someone to purchase, store and replenish
- Teaching materials – what to choose and how to use it.

Things to do:

- Regular policy meetings with elders (or deacons); accountability is vital
- Programme planning meeting with all those helping
- Publicity and letters to parents – it may be the only contact with some
- Record-keeping – attendance, ages, home contact numbers, special health factors
- Finance – do you charge subs? Is there a budget? How are expenses claimed?
- Training sessions for leaders – do you arrange these 'in-house' or are you using an external agency?
- Prayer – the whole church must be involved.

Use these as a checklist to look at the needs of the children's work in your church.

 How can you involve the whole church in prayer?

HOW WELL ARE WE DOING?

Even when young people's work is going well, it is easy to lose sight of why we're doing it and to become purely pragmatic. Assuming you have thought through the aims as outlined in the Introduction, regular review and prayer is needed on many issues. Some of these principles or factors may pull in different directions. Asking the questions below will help in the process of regular review…

- How does youth work fit within the overall church strategy for outreach (assuming you have one!)?
- Have you considered church priorities in the light of limited resources, so that youth work is neither neglected nor sacrosanct?
- Within the youth work itself, is there a clear strategy for children to progress through the different groups and activities as they grow older? It is easy to lose children at every transition.
- Do you review tactics as well as strategy? Which games do the children enjoy most? (How would you find out?) What situations or combinations of children may be difficult to handle?
- Is the balance right between fun activities and spiritual input?

- Does your planning take account of particular times of pressure in young people's lives (such as a change of school or taking SATs or GCSEs)?
- Are you aware of the moral and legal responsibility of dealing with other people's children? Does your church have a Child Protection Policy in place?
- Do leaders know what is expected of them? Is there training provided?
- How do you expect children to respond to the gospel message? What difficulties arise with children from non-Christian homes when they respond to the gospel challenge they hear from a church children's club?
- What contact do you have with parents? How could you make this more meaningful?

THINK IT THROUGH

1. How do you get the whole church involved in prayer for youth work in your church?

2. Review your Child Protection Policy. Are your leaders implementing it?

3. Discuss the pros and cons of having subs.

4. What opportunities exist for young people in your church to meet other Christian youth groups? Can you create these opportunities if they're not there already?

FOLLOW IT UP

Would there ever be a case for setting someone aside in your church in a full or part-time capacity as a youth worker? In an age of limited resources, think through the pros and cons.

CHILDREN'S AND YOUTH WORK

DOING THE TALK

THERE IS AN IMMENSE VARIETY in the different opportunities we get to help youngsters at meetings, so we can't cover everything here. But there are some 'hints and tips' that can guide us whenever we are given the chance to speak.

CONTEXT

Here are four issues you need to resolve before you open your mouth…

- **Be clear about what you are being asked to do.** Don't be afraid to ask what may seem obvious questions so that you are fully aware of what is planned and how you fit in with the overall objectives.
- **Do what you are asked to do.** There is always a great temptation to go beyond the task assigned to us. In all normal circumstances it is important to remember this insight, and not cause irritation or embarrassment by overriding it.
- **Keep to time.** This is a special and much-needed underlining of point 2 above. The speaker who was asked to address 12-16 year-olds for 20 minutes but who took one hour and 20 minutes didn't do anyone any favours.
- **Be sensitive to your surroundings.** We want to build bridges to our hearers, not erect barriers. Adapting to our audience will involve adjustment on our part. Forcing everything into 'Sunday service' mode is not what is called for!

Look back over the ground we covered in the first Unit of Track 4 and then brainstorm the kinds of ways in which you might have to adjust to speak at the following events:

1. *A lively school CU meeting.*
2. *A baby's thanksgiving service.*
3. *A children's carol service with lots of non-Christian children and their parents present.*
4. *A dads and lads five-a-side evening with epilogue.*
5. *A school assembly after the funeral of a youngster.*

COMMUNICATION

MATERIAL

Generally speaking, if the talk is aimed at non-Christians then to speak topically is the best way to build bridges of communication with your hearers.

Read John 4:1-26

Look at the way Jesus engages with a non-Christian in this passage. If that's how he deals with an unbelieving adult, we should be every bit as creative when telling the gospel to children and young people. The Samaritan woman's main concern is water. Jesus uses this to present the gospel to her.

1. What are the main concerns of children and teenagers today?

2. How can we use these as a launch pad for presenting the gospel?

If the listeners are mainly Christian and the aim is to build them up, then opening up a passage will be a better way of helping them to get to grips with the Bible's message.

METHOD

In looking at how we present material, there are many important points covered in other parts of the course, but think about these three big ideas when communicating with youngsters.

In your group, brainstorm to find one key word that says it all for each heading.

1. You – *which word is going to describe you and your attitude as you present the gospel?*

2. Them – *which word is going to describe the way you engage them?*

3. The Message – *which word is going to describe what you say?*

We can make the message clearer by using tools that particularly help children. They love stories, and respond to vivid illustrations which adults may regard as 'o-t-t'. Humour, even rather juvenile humour, appeals to them. Contemporary illustrations work best. But remember, 'contemporary' does not mean to them what it means to you. *'Back in '66, when England won the World Cup...'* might as well be 1066 as far as they are concerned! Material that just interests you – *'on the Ten o'clock News last night...'* will not connect with them. Think of other ways of making things stick.

CHILDREN

Both in your preparation and the delivery of a talk, it is important that you don't forget that they are children. What should you take into account? Here are a few 'tension points' to bear in mind...

- **Overestimating/underestimating their capacity.** Too difficult and they switch off; too easy... and they still switch off! It takes skill, which can only come with experience, and as a result of knowing your youngsters, to get this one right. Be careful with the vocabulary you use, the length of time you speak for, the concepts you include – can you explain them? – the life-applications you make, and tone of voice and 'body language' you adopt. Remember a couple of rules of thumb...
  - Children usually come up or down to what you expect. So it is better to aim for a good standard of content than just put up with the minimum possible
  - Simple things, learned well, stick best. Which adverts do you recall

from your youth? Aren't they mostly the ones with catchy slogans and tunes – 'a Mars a day...'?

- **All the same/all very different.** You may be tempted to lump them all together as 'children' and, in one way, that is right – they will all go through similar phases of growing up. But each one is very different and you mustn't expect them all to be interested in sports, or pop music, or fashion, or anything else, in the same way. And to make a child feel even more different by pinpointing some trait that is unusual or stands out is equally unhelpful.
- **Putting them at ease/keeping sensible discipline.** Sometimes the context will help you. For example, school assemblies are often 'well patrolled' by good staff, and you can connect well with the children by being relaxed and easy-going. But in other situations that same approach will lead youngsters to start misbehaving, thinking that you have given them the cue for silly or downright difficult behaviour.

On the subject of discipline...
1. What have you done in the past with problems of discipline?
2. Would you handle them differently now?

Finally there are three other factors which need to be remembered concerning the young people to whom you are about to speak...

- **The surroundings they come from.** Some will be harbouring memories of sad and difficult home lives which will make them emotionally vulnerable or poorly-behaved. Some may need specialist help that is not within your own expertise.
- **The culture they live in.** A talk should do its best to 'connect' with this, not just on a superficial level only, but addressing their deepest fears, interests, joys and aspirations.
- **The future they have ahead of them.** Generally, they have a lot more time ahead of them than you have, so they are more future-oriented than you are. How can you capitalise on this in the different contexts you are in, capturing their dreams, visions, and longings... **for Christ**? (See 2 Corinthians 10:5)

How can you stay in touch with children's and young people's culture?

CHALLENGES

Behind each talk there should be a passionate and enthusiastic desire to communicate your aim. In every talk, you are calling young people to either or both of the following steps...

- **To convert to Christ.** This is not about browbeating or manipulating responses, but recognising that the most wonderful thing that can ever happen to anyone is to come to know Christ. You will vary how you put this all the time but, at its heart, Christianity is not about rules, or history lessons, or entertaining stories, but about the right *relationship* with Jesus Christ. How they can come into this relationship is an important part of talking to youngsters.

• **To commit to Christ.** After conversion there needs to be an ongoing challenge, and encouragement, to keep following the Lord. To keep telling them that the Lord will help them by his Holy Spirit is so important because 'growing up' can be such an overwhelming experience (you only have to ask adults *'Who wants to be 15 again?'* to find out!). Inadequacy is often the dominant adolescent feeling.

THINK IT THROUGH

1. How do you think music can help communicate to young children, pre-adolescents, and teenagers?

2. List some things that should be avoided when you're talking to children and young people? Do you say any of these things?

FOLLOW IT UP

Put together the outline programme for an 11s-14s evening on the subject of anger and violence. Think of a good title.

CHURCH LEADERSHIP

DEVELOPING AN ELDERSHIP

LEADERSHIP ALWAYS IMPLIES that someone is following. At one level, a good leader is simply someone others want to follow. Perhaps those of us in leadership need to think more often about what it means for people to follow us.

1. Try this scenario. You and some friends are off on holiday. The destination sounds idyllic and you can't wait to get there. But you don't know the way. Fear not, Mike does. And he offers to take the lead – the rest of you can follow. Discuss the range of emotions you are likely to experience on the journey when you discover that Mike is up ahead driving:
   - a 25-year-old truck, loaded well beyond its limit
   - an Aston Martin
2. How do these unlikely events bear on the way church members may feel about following us?

TWO HEADS ARE BETTER THAN ONE

These days, every part of church life is coming under intense scrutiny. We are asking questions about the way we worship … the way we evangelise … our commitment to world mission … and the way our churches are led.

For many of us, the traditional pattern of church leadership handed down from the previous generation included one pastor and a team of supportive helpers (deacons). Since the 1970s this arrangement has come under increasing challenge and there have been significant moves towards a plurality of elders.

The Bible says much more about elders than deacons. In this Unit, we will be concentrating on eldership, although this may not be the label you use for the leaders in your church.

Study the following Scriptures:
- Acts 6:1-4
- Acts 14:23
- Acts 20:17-28

1. What do they suggest about the leadership of local churches?
2. What responsibilities do elders have in the Acts of the Apostles?
3. In the light of this, what bearing does 1 Timothy 2:11-15 have on who qualifies to be an elder?
4. Does the evidence suggest that the plurality of elders is a matter of cultural setting, personal style or biblical authority?

ADVANTAGES OF PLURAL ELDERSHIP

Church leaders are often rugged individualists who don't make natural team players. With that thought in mind, discuss the practical benefits of a plurality of elders.

1. What are the advantages of a plural eldership?
2. What are the dangers of a one-man leadership?

JOB SPECIFICATION

Read 1 Peter 5:1-3

1. *Comparing Scripture with Scripture reveals that terms like pastor, elder and overseer (bishop) simply describe different aspects of the same ministry. Discuss what each title might suggest?*
   - *Pastor...*
   - *Elder...*
   - *Overseer...*
2. *Are all elders required to be preachers? Check out the following Scriptures in arriving at an answer:*
   - *1 Timothy 3:2-7*
   - *Titus 1:9*
   - *1 Peter 5:1-3*
   - *Acts 20:28*

The ability to teach... to encourage... to refute doesn't necessarily imply public preaching. What every elder must be able to do is to use God's word to nurture, guide and direct each member of the church.

Look at 1 Timothy 5:17

1. What are all elders to be able to do?
2. What are some elders to focus on especially?

Rather than insist on a one-dimensional approach to leadership, the Bible speaks of a rounded ministry which reflects the work of the ultimate pastor in every church, the Lord Jesus himself. We can think of him as Prophet, Priest and King. These ministries were not separate in our Lord's life and they are not separate within a church leadership team. He is the supreme example of leadership.

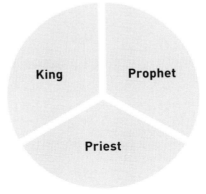

How are these three ministries reflected in our human leadership?

MAKING IT WORK

 Read Ephesians 4:11-16

 Every leader needs objectives. From this passage, how would you define the objectives of the eldership in your local church?

THINK IT THROUGH

1. How often is church order taught in your church?
2. If you were a local church leader, what obstacles would stand in the way of your acceptance of a team ministry?
3. How are the ministries of prophet, priest and king being exercised in your church?
4. Are certain groups of people in your church not being ministered to in the Ephesians 4:12-13 sense? Why? What can you do about it?
5. How do you try to keep the balance between the demands of serving in the church with the other demands of everyday life? Check back over the material you covered in Unit 3.4, Keeping the balance.

FOLLOW IT UP

 Imagine that your church has hit a glass ceiling. After prayerful discussion, the elders conclude that you have no strategy to handle growth. You have lots of people working very hard, but you have not yet found a way of turning talk about gifts into action. Prepare an outline paper for your next imaginary elders' meeting to chart a way forward.

Use a table like the one on the right to break the work of the whole church down into manageable teams and define in general terms what the responsibility of each team should be. One or two examples are given to help you.

Next time, discuss the advantages of this approach to church leadership...

Team	Coordinator	Members	Responsibilities
Service planning			• plan outline for services in consultation with preacher(s). • arrange suitable people to lead the service, pray, read the Bible, talk to children, give mission update. • liaise with music group.
Evangelism planning			• develop strategic plan. • plan and coordinate annual programme of events. • provide training. • liaise with catering team.

CHURCH LEADERSHIP

DEVELOPING RELATIONSHIPS

LEADERSHIP IS NOT about leaders, but about the people being led. The aim of this Unit is to help you to see how relationships are an essential part of achieving the goal of church life.

Split into two groups. Both groups should build the tallest stable Lego tower possible in five minutes. But … no talking is permitted in Group 1; there are no such restrictions in Group 2.

How did it go? Communication is the key.

THE RELATIONSHIP BETWEEN ELDERS

The ideal is for the eldership to be composed of people with different temperaments, gifts, social backgrounds and life experiences. You need to learn to love one another. The shepherding of the church begins with the example you give as elders. The apostles often appeal to their own conduct as an example to the churches. See 1 Thessalonians 2:10.

LOVE EACH OTHER

Think of the time the Lord Jesus spent teaching the disciples how to relate to each other. One analysis of this *Doubtful Dozen* (below) indicates just what a handful they were.

The Doubtful Dozen

It is the staff's opinion that most of your nominees are lacking in background, education and vocational aptitude for the type of enterprise you are undertaking. They do not have the team concept. We would recommend that you continue your search for persons of experience in managerial ability and proven capability.

- **Simon Peter** is emotionally unstable and given to fits of temper.
- **Andrew** has absolutely no qualities of leadership.
- The two brothers, **James** and **John**, the sons of Zebedee, place personal interest above company loyalty.
- **Thomas** demonstrates a questioning attitude that would tend to undermine morale.
- We feel it is our duty to tell you that **Matthew** has been blacklisted by the Greater Jerusalem Better Business Bureau.
- **James**, son of Alphaeus, and **Thaddaeus**, definitely have radical leanings, and they both registered a high score on the manic-depressive scale.
- One of the candidates, however, shows great potential. He is a man of ability and resourcefulness, meets people well, has a keen business mind and has contacts in high places. He is highly motivated, ambitious and responsible. We recommend **Judas Iscariot** as your controller and right-hand man.

We wish you success in your new venture.

From Frogs in Cream, Stephen Gaukroger and Nick Mercer, London: Scripture Union, 1990.

Study the following Scriptures:
- *Matthew 18:21-22*

•*John 13:34-35*
•*John 15:12-13*

What lessons emerge?

1. What tensions threatened the unity between the Twelve?
2. What tensions may exist within a modern day eldership?

What do you learn from Paul's treatment of his fellow workers?
• *Romans 16:3-16*
• *Philippians 2:19-30*

Paul is so good at creating a climate of encouragement. Perhaps two key words in every leader's vocabulary should be **Thank you**.

RECOGNISE AND REJOICE IN EACH OTHER'S GIFTS

A full-time elder is in the best position to know what is going on in the church and it is probably natural for him to take the lead in a general way. But it is by no means the case that preaching elders are the best leaders. Some are hopeless organisers; others are inept at leading church business meetings. We need to learn to submit to one another in love and gratitude to the Lord.

When an individual elder has been invited to take responsibility for a particular ministry, give him scope to guide that work and to develop it in his own way.

WATCH OVER EACH OTHER'S SPIRITUAL LIVES

Who pastors the pastors? In theory, a plural eldership where there is love and mutual appreciation will help to provide the answer.

1. What particular spiritual dangers do elders face?
2. What warning signs may suggest that an elder is struggling in his walk with God?

THE RELATIONSHIP BETWEEN ELDERS AND DEACONS

First and foremost, elders and deacons are not outside the church, looking in; neither are they above the church, looking down. They are members of Christ's body, called to serve him within it. All leadership in the local church is deacon-ing, in the sense that it is always ministry undertaken by servants.

Read Acts 6:1-7

Although the seven men in this passage are not specifically called deacons, they are often seen as the diaconate in embryo.

1. Why are they appointed?

2. Why don't the apostles (acting as elders in the Jerusalem church) take personal charge of the relief programme?

3. Does this mean that they let go of all responsibility for relief? See Acts 11:30.

Look again at the following familiar Scriptures:

• Philippians 1:1

• 1 Timothy 3:1-13

You may be interested to discover that whereas elders are often mentioned on their own, the New Testament normally refers to deacons in conjunction with elders. In simple terms, the job of the deacons is to help the elders to do theirs.

Look over what was said above about the relationships between elders and then discuss…

1. What does that imply for the working relationship between the elders and deacons?

2. What, in your church, is the best way for elders and deacons to coordinate their ministries?

THE RELATIONSHIP BETWEEN ELDERS AND CHURCH MEMBERS

Remember that your church is made up of volunteers and that relationships are the glue that holds it together. Friendship is the key to retaining members.

Read 1 Peter 5:1-5

1. How does Peter address the elders of the churches? Why does that sound strange coming from Peter?

2. What, from this passage, are the hallmarks of true pastoral care?

3. Compare verse 5 with John 13:1-17. Why is Peter's imagery so striking?

4. If you are an elder in your church, how did you perceive the eldership before you joined?

Healthy relationships are two-way!

Brainstorm ways in which church members can encourage their leaders. Do it now – you've got the Lord firmly on your side. See Hebrews 13:17.

DISCIPLINING AN ELDER

Leaders are always in the public eye at church – and that makes them vulnerable. Inevitably, they are exposed to gossip and criticism. For the most part, they should follow the example of our Master and not retaliate (1 Peter 2:23). But when serious accusations are made against an elder, his fellow-elders must step in to protect his reputation and/or the reputation of the church.

Tragically, there will be occasions when serious accusations prove to be well founded.

Read 1 Timothy 5:19-20

1. What facts of life are implicit in what Paul writes here?

2. When should the other elders and the church take accusations seriously?

3. Paul says that those 'found guilty' are to be rebuked publicly. Discuss what range of options the church may have available. Remember Unit 3.2 Meeting the mark. An elder is to be **above reproach** or **blameless**. See 1 Timothy 3:2.That doesn't mean **morally perfect**. It means that if I take the platform on Sunday, will there be anything about my personal life which comes to your mind and gets in the way of your receiving my ministry?

THINK IT THROUGH

1. If elders are unable to agree among themselves on a vital matter, what can they do? How can they present their differences to the church?

2. Between them, the elders need to know everyone in the congregation. How can they do this?

3. Do a quick brainstorm – how can we build a relational component into every meeting at church?

FOLLOW IT UP

Take a look at Tychicus. If you remember the story, Paul is imprisoned in Rome. He sends Tychicus to Colossae with Onesimus, the runaway slave and two letters – one to the whole church, the other to Philemon. His instructions go something like this, 'Now, I want you to go to Colossae and sort this out for me. It's important and I'm depending on you'. Tychicus is not a leader; he is an empowered follower. Look at Colossians 4:7-8 and identify five qualities that make Tychicus an ideal ambassador.

CHURCH LEADERSHIP

DEVELOPING VISION

WE LOOKED AT Ephesians 4:11–16 in Unit 5.4, Developing an eldership. In that passage, Paul sets out the New Testament model of church. It's about:

- leaders who prepare God's people for works of service – that's every-member ministry
- a community of love, acceptance and forgiveness which encourages growth – that's relationship; and
- people with a purpose – that's vision.

In this Unit, we will look at how leaders can communicate this sense of purpose to the members of the church.

A group of monks went to a monastery for a weekend retreat. It was Friday evening, and they all joined together for *Complin*, a service of prayers at the end of the day. There were four different orders represented at the retreat – Dominicans, Benedictines, Franciscans and Jesuits. Soon after the service began, the lights went out and pitch darkness enveloped the monastery. The Dominicans prayed on, oblivious to the darkness, as they knew the service by heart. The Benedictines fell to their knees and prayed fervently that light might be restored to the monastery, so that they could follow their service book and continue with *Complin*. The Franciscans sat back in their pews and launched into a profound philosophical discussion as to the relative virtues of darkness and light. The Jesuits went out and fixed the fuse.

We need people who know what needs to be done. See Ephesians 5:15-17.

1. Look at Ephesians 4:12-13 again. What, according to Paul in this passage, is the point of church?

2. Do you have a church mission statement? If not, try to formulate a single sentence that summarises the raison d'être of your church.

FOCUSING THE VISION

Remember, it is Christ's church, not ours. It isn't our job to create his purposes, but rather to discover them and fulfil them.

How do these verses from Ephesians contribute to your understanding of Paul's vision for the church?

- *1:22-23*
- *2:8-10*
- *2:19-22*
- *3:14-21*
- *4:1-6*
- *5:18-20*
- *6:10-18*

As you formulate your ideas, look for answers to these four questions:

1. Why does the church exist?
*2. What are we to **be** as a church?*
*3. What are we to **do** as a church?*
4. How are we to do it?

In his book, *The Purpose Driven Church*[1], Rick Warren suggests that we should ask four questions of every purpose statement:

....

[1]   The Purpose Driven Church, Rick Warren, Zondervan 1995 p100.

- Is it biblical? Does it reflect the purposes of Christ, the head of the Church?
- Is it specific? Does it force you to focus your energy?
- Is it transferable? Can it be remembered and passed on?
- Is it measurable? Is your purpose statement about activities, or about results? How do you know that you are achieving the goals mentioned in the purpose statement?

How does your church's purpose statement measure up?

COMMUNICATING THE VISION

Read Nehemiah 4:6-15

Look over the work you did on Nehemiah in Unit 3.5, *Leading the flock*.

In the story of rebuilding the wall around Jerusalem, the people become discouraged halfway through the project and want to give up.

1. What pressures build up in their minds?

2. What steps does Nehemiah take to keep them on task?

3. What lessons can we learn for our church from Nehemiah's leadership?

If leaders need to communicate the vision as often as once a month (compare Nehemiah 4:6 with 6:15 – that's every 26 days in his case), we need a range of tools to help us to do it. Here are some ideas:

- **Teach the church about the church regularly – with passion and enthusiasm.** Remember what Paul says about it in Ephesians 3:10. The best textbook on church growth is the Bible. And keep at it. Don't assume that a one-off sermon or a single series will set the direction of your church forever.
- **Work at simple sound bites.** There is great power in slogans, mottos and pithy sayings – they will probably be remembered long after the sermons are forgotten. Remember some of the great slogans behind the Reformation. Work on some now. Here are two to get you started:
- *Saved to serve*
- *The main thing is to keep the main thing the main thing*
- **Spread the word through the various groups in the church.** Everyone should be pulling in the same direction – or singing from the same slide!
- **Follow Nehemiah's example.** Always talk in terms of clear, concrete steps that will enable your congregation to realise the vision.
- **Make it personal** – through your home groups and youth groups, for instance. Let individuals know what they can do to make the vision a reality.

• **Use stories.** Jesus was a master at using simple human-interest stories to communicate his vision. Provide regular opportunities for folk to share testimony of how God has been fulfilling the vision through their ministries.

Nehemiah reminds us that the vision of any church will fade with time unless we reinforce it. Keep saying the same thing in different ways – then you will eventually capture everyone's attention. Generally speaking, the kind of lifechanges we are looking for don't come at moments of spiritual crisis, but from the drip-drip of consistent exposure to the same message.

DELIVERING THE VISION

It has been said that there are five main thrusts to church life:
• evangelism
• worship
• fellowship
• Bible teaching
• social conscience

Take a look at the table below adapted from *The Purpose Driven Church* and fill in the gaps.

Most churches emphasise what their leaders feel strongly about and neglect whatever their leaders are less passionate about. Unless you set up structures which serve to balance these five goals, your church will simply reflect the gifts and passions of the leaders. That's why Paul speaks of the maturing church as a community in which each member plays his or her part (Ephesians 4:16).

	The primary focus of this church	The leaders' role in this church	People's role in this church
The Soul-winning church			Witnesses
The Experiencing God church			
The Building Relationships church	Fellowship		
The Bible Teaching church			
The Social Conscience church			Activists
The Purpose Driven church		Facilitators	

*Look back to the **Follow it up** exercise at the end of Unit 5.4. How do the teams you identified in that Unit reflect the five main goals of the maturing church?*

VISION AND THE BUSINESS MEETING

Church meetings should be one of the most precious worship opportunities in our life together. Here the core of the church comes together in the presence of the Lord to seek his will for the growth of the gospel in our area and beyond. Try to strip out the administrative trivia from the business meeting and make it a strategic opportunity for sharing the vision.

1. How do we reach decisions when we meet together?

2. Traditionally, many churches adopt a system of (secret) voting. Discuss the pros and cons of this approach.

We need to take seriously the work of the Holy Spirit in leading a church to unanimity of mind as well as of heart. It requires members and leaders alike to be submissive to the Spirit and to each other. It requires the elders to work patiently in leading the church to a common mind.

Decisions! Decisions!

- **Many matters are purely administrative.** Do they need to be discussed in this forum at all? If they do, ask the responsible person to report on progress, give opportunity for questions and gauge the general feeling of the meeting without making heavy weather of voting procedures.
- **Other matters are urgent and require immediate action.** You don't hold a consultation if a blind man is walking towards the edge of a cliff!
- **Some matters are of strategic importance to the future life of the church.** Flag up well in advance when you are going to be considering these kinds of issue. Why not make outline copies of the leaders' meeting agenda available to the church at large? When it comes to the members' meeting, take care to show how your initial conclusions seek to serve the church's vision. Allow plenty of time for discussion on the understanding that views, not decisions, are being sought at this point.

This may facilitate freedom of expression and help people to avoid feeling that they need to take sides. It also affords the elders the opportunity to listen to several different points of view and discuss the matter with individuals outside the meeting before it comes to crunch-time. At this point, one member with a good case may be instrumental in making you think again. The ultimate aim should always be unanimity.

Don't seek a decision until everyone has had the opportunity to express their opinion and you have had the chance to weigh counter-arguments carefully and to address them honestly. Where people are known to disagree with the final decision, take care to minister to them. Riding roughshod over minority groups is not part of the life of a church where the spirit of Jesus Christ prevails.

Discuss the pros and cons of this third approach to decision-making in church.

THINK IT THROUGH

1. Look back at the table on page 40.
   Where does your church's focus lie? In which areas do you need to grow the church's ministry?

2. Discuss the broad outline for a sermon series on God's blueprint for the church.

3. How can you engage members in a way that draws them into wanting to deliver the vision?

4. What can elders do to make the business meeting a more positive experience?

FOLLOW IT UP

Prepare some ideas for an away-day which your church leaders might spend together developing a sense of vision.

PREACHING A SERMON

DEFINING THE BIG IDEA

THE AIM of the first two Preaching Units is to introduce you to the work of preaching – and take you step by step through the process of preparing a sermon[1]. 'Forget it – preaching has had its day!' That's a comment we often hear. The critics suggest that preaching is about as effective as trying to fill a row of milk bottles by throwing a pail of water over them.

---

1 Many of the ideas in these Units are drawn from *Expository Preaching —Principles & Practice*, Haddon W Robinson, IVP.

1. How do you respond to that kind of criticism?
2. Why are these such difficult days for preaching and preachers?

GET INTO THE BIBLE

Read Acts 15:6-11

How would you set verse 7 out in the form of a diagram (already started below)?

GOD made a CHOICE that

This verse tells us that God is totally committed to preaching. How will that thought lift and encourage the preacher?

THE IMPORTANCE OF PREPARATION

It is tempting to think that the Holy Spirit will give us the words we need on the spur of the moment. He can ... and at times, he does. But God won't subsidise laziness. See 2 Timothy 2:15.

What are the dangers of using your Quiet Time to search for sermons?

Read Ecclesiastes 12:9-12

Here we have the Preacher on preaching. Notice three things:
• the hard work behind the scenes, searching out material
• the care he takes in presenting the message
• the impact it has on the lives of its hearers.

STEPS IN PREPARING A SERMON

STAGE I – WHICH PASSAGE?

Think about the kind of considerations that will determine which passage you choose.

STAGE 2 – WHAT DOES THE PASSAGE SAY?

What does it mean...
• in its immediate context?
• in the context of the Book?
• in the context of the overall message of the Bible?

Read and re-read it in two or three different translations – the ESV for accuracy ... perhaps a more dynamic translation like the NIV for creating a vivid impression in your mind.

Read Psalm 98

1. What kind of passage is it?

2. Refer back to Setting the Scene at the start of Track 1, Understanding the Bible and produce a quick list of the kinds of literature to be found in the Bible. Narrative passages will probably be longer than, say, a parable. And the type of literature will affect the way you approach the passage.

How is dealing with Law different from the way we would treat a poem or a parable?

Use the tools available to you. Ask your tutor about the kinds of concordances, dictionaries and commentaries they find helpful.

Look for the main teaching point of the passage – the Big Idea. Keep refining the Big Idea throughout the whole process. Imagine someone calls you up in the week to say that they can't be in church on Sunday morning. They ask, 'What are you going to preach on?' By this point, you need to be able to sum up your sermon in one crisp sentence.

STAGE 3 – HOW DOES THE PASSAGE TEACH THE BIG IDEA?

Keep asking questions like How? What? Why? When? Where? and Who?

Read James 1:5-8

It's obvious that this is a passage on wisdom, but read it in its immediate context:

• *where is this wisdom to be found?*

• *how can we get it?*

• *when do we need it?*

• *what might stand in the way of us receiving it?*

As a group, come up with a short sharp sentence which captures the Big Idea.

For more help on interacting with the text, see Unit 4.1, *Using the Bible.*

STAGE 4 – HOW DO I GET FROM A TEXT TO A SERMON?

We are beginning to distil our study now. So far, we've concentrated on the passage, but what about the congregation to whom this passage must speak? Start to ask some questions on their behalf:

• What does this mean? It may be obvious to you, but what about that person in the back row who has only just started coming to church?

• Is it true? Can I believe it? People who believe the Bible often ignore this question; but we do so at our peril. Does the writer answer it in the passage itself?

• What difference does it make? What should I do differently because I have heard this word from God?

We're now reaching the point where we can sum up the passage in one sharp, pithy sentence. We may distrust politicians and their facility for speaking in sound bites, but we shouldn't underestimate the value of the apt one-liner.

STAGE 5 – WHAT'S THE POINT?

Good question. What's the point of:

- Studying a map? To reach a destination.
- Reading a recipe? To bake a cake.
- Preaching a sermon? To change people's lives.

Remember, the Bible has not been given as a book of systematic theology to be understood, but as a manual for life to be obeyed. The purpose must come out of the passage. We must not be like the preacher who, after preaching on Cain and Abel, concluded with: 'And now a word about baptism!'

THINK IT THROUGH

1. What does Paul say in 2 Timothy 3:14-17 about:

- *the significance of Scripture being Godbreathed?*
- *the purpose of Scripture – from start to finish?*
- *the changes the Bible is intended to produce in the life of the believer?*

2. Looking at the immediate context – what bearing is all this intended to have on the preaching ministry of Timothy?

FOLLOW IT UP

Take the Book of Hebrews. The author seems to be writing to persuade a group of newly converted Hebrew Christians that, despite all appearances to the contrary, the door on Old Testament worship is now firmly shut; they cannot go back. He knows that their emotional ties with the temple and everything it has stood for go very deep. Scan the first 10 chapters before your next session to see how carefully he makes the case that the gospel is true, and that they must believe it. Discuss your findings next time.

PREACHING A SERMON

REFINING THE BIG IDEA

REMEMBER, the aim of these three Units is to introduce you to the work of preaching – and take you step by step through the process of preparing a sermon.

STAGE 6 – HOW DO I ACCOMPLISH THE PURPOSE?

By this stage, we know what we are going to preach — and why. Now we've got to work at how. What shape is this sermon going to take? At this point, we start to work on the outline.

A clear outline won't guarantee a good sermon, but what will it achieve?

Read Ephesians 1:3-14

Here is Paul explaining to the Ephesian Christians how they should respond to God. Look for the key word here – you'll find it in verses 6, 12 and 14. How does that help you to see what the passage is about?

Now go through the passage again and see how Paul develops the theme. At each step along the way, the reasons for praising God become more and more compelling until we finally want to burst into song with him in verse 3.

STAGE 7 – SEASON TO TASTE

Illustrations are a vital part of every sermon – why?

Beware of two dangers especially:
- don't use illustrations that draw attention away from the Big Idea. You don't look at windows, you look through them.
- don't use personal stories from your own ministry in the church — people won't confide in you about their problems if they fear that they'll show up as an illustration next time you preach.

Where can you get good illustrations? They are everywhere — incidents in your own life… news items in the press… illustrations from the movies (for example, *Saving Private Ryan* is not only a powerful film against glorifying war, it also asks the question – *is he worth saving*? God's answer to that kind of question is the cross). Get into the habit of looking out for them. And keep a notebook handy, so that you can jot them down when you find them.

STAGE 8 – PLAN YOUR TAKE-OFF AND LANDING

The hardest elements of any flight are the take-off and the landing. You wouldn't trust the pilot who left them to chance. Preaching is not so very different.

- **Introductions** Remember, you're up against a fallen congregation and an enemy of souls. So, make the first ten seconds count. A sermon on suffering might start like this:

'Where was God at [date and time of recent disaster]?'

That kind of arresting question will certainly grab people's attention…

- either they have asked it themselves and are keen to hear what the Bible has to say
- or they're asking it now and you've got to come up with the answer. What's the point? You want to build a relationship with your congregation … and introduce what you want to say to them. You've got something important from God's word which they need to hear and upon which they must act. Two more don'ts:
- don't spend so long spreading the table that people lose their appetites! One famous preacher is regularly told by the organisers of a conference that if he can't get through his introduction in the first twenty minutes, he won't be asked to speak again.
- don't promise more than you can deliver from the passage — setting light to a cannon to fire a pea is a waste of gunpowder.
- **Conclusions** The conclusion may come last in the sermon and it's last here, but it certainly shouldn't come last in your preparation. Everything else is working up to this point. A Hollywood producer once said that for a movie to be a success, it must start with an earthquake and work up to a climax.

What's the conclusion for? Discuss some ideas in your group.

Above all, the preacher's conclusion must be like the barrister's summing up – you are appealing for a verdict. By now, the congregation has seen the whole argument of the passage. You've explained it and illustrated it and applied it. Now they need to know exactly what they need to do about it…

- What difference does this passage make to my life?
- Am I willing, with God's help, to make that difference?

Think of some different ways in which you can bring a sermon to a conclusion.

PREACHING THE SERMON

You will find lots of helpful advice on speaking in public in the next Unit on *Presenting the Big Idea.*

THINK IT THROUGH

In this Unit, we have been planning to preach a 'traditional' sermon – a monologue from the pulpit. But explore the ministries of great pulpit preachers and you'll discover that they use a wide range of other teaching methods. As evangelical Christians, we must be word based without being pulpit-bound.

1. Think about the ministry of Paul and jot down some of the methods he used to teach the gospel.

2. *Think about ways of developing the sermon:*
- *What are the pros and cons of having three ten-minute talks rather than one thirty minute sermon in, say, a family service?*
- *Would there be merit in a well-directed question to the congregation after the sermon has been preached?*

3. *Looking back over this Unit, preparing a sermon may seem rather a cerebral activity. Real preaching is about the heart as well as the head; it inflames the heart as well as informing the mind. Pray now that the preaching you hear and the preaching you undertake is full of grace and full of glory – what Dr Martyn Lloyd-Jones would call,* **Logic on fire***.*

FOLLOW IT UP

With regard to the sermons coming up in the next week or two, listen especially to the introductions and conclusions. Which do you find particularly effective, and why?

PREACHING A SERMON

PRESENTING THE BIG IDEA

THE AIM of these three Units is to get you thinking about the work of preaching. Now that you have identified the Big Idea in your study passage, how do you get it across? In this final Unit, you will be looking at communication skills in general.

The story is told of the Scouts who knocked on the front door of a large country house looking for work. They were instructed to go round to the back and whitewash the inside of the porch. On their return to collect the money, one of the boys commented in passing, 'Oh, by the way, it wasn't a Porsche, it was a Ferrari!' The cost of poor communication can be very high

Think about some of the basic issues at stake:
- *What is the point of communication?*
- *Who is involved in any piece of communication?*
- *What factors are going to help or hinder the communication process?*
- *With these points in mind, produce a diagram to illustrate the dynamics of communication.*

GET INTO THE BIBLE

Read 1 Thessalonians 1:4 – 2:13

LIVING YOUR MESSAGE

Our lives are our Number One means of communication. Someone once defined preaching as the presentation of truth through personality.

How do you see that here in Paul's gospel ministry in Thessalonica?
- *How does Paul view the gospel he has been commissioned to communicate?*
- *How does the gospel shape his own way of life?*
- *When Paul presents the gospel, what words describe the way he does it?*

Whenever you are given the opportunity to speak for God – whether in a prepared talk or in an off-the cuff conversation, live what you say. Feel it deeply.

LEARNING TO LISTEN

1. How did the Thessalonians respond when Paul brought the truth to them?
2. Who communicates with you? What is it about them which gets through to you? Discuss your experience with the rest of the group.

Start listening with new ears to the sermons and Bible talks you hear. Are there weaknesses in the presentation you can identify and determine to avoid? Do you daydream? If so, why? Is it something to do with you? And, if so, what can you do to change it? Or is it the fault of the speaker?

When a preacher once motioned to a deacon to wake up someone who had nodded off in the back row, the deacon said: 'You sent him to sleep – you wake him up!'

Take notes, even if you throw them away afterwards. The very act of committing your thoughts to paper will aid your own ability to learn.

Careful listening will pay dividends in two ways:
- You will develop your own skills in public speaking
- When teaching a small class, you will have a much clearer idea of where your participants are coming from.

LOOKING UP AND SPEAKING OUT

Read John 7:37-44

It's the Feast of Tabernacles and Jerusalem is buzzing with eager worshippers. How does Jesus seize the attention of his hearers?

Think about some of the best public speakers you know. What makes them what they are? Discuss your findings.

ORGANISING YOUR MATERIAL

Look back over *Introductions* and *Conclusions* in the last Unit, *Refining the big idea*. The key points in every talk are:

- **the beginning** – how are you going to win your hearers' attention? Why should they spend the next twenty minutes listening to you? Tell a story or ask a provocative question.

- **the end** – many speakers are like trainee pilots who don't know how to land their plane. Plan your touchdown from the start. Summarise the one main lesson you've set out to teach and make sure people understand what you want them to do about it.

Read John 4:4-26

Jesus' discussion with the woman at the well is a marvellous piece of one to one communication.

Identify from the passage how Jesus takes each of the following steps and then put them in the right order.

- *Test commitment*
- *Keep to the point*
- *Arouse interest*
- *Establish common ground*
- *Challenge to change*
- *Carry the argument forward*

USING NOTES

The simple rule is – use notes with which you are comfortable. Exceptional preachers like C H Spurgeon and Dr Martyn Lloyd-Jones both used brief notes.

Discuss some of the pros and the cons of brief notes compared with a fuller manuscript.

If you speak from a full manuscript, learn to take in a sentence or two at a glance so that you can keep your eyes on those listening. Try to use words that people won't be expecting. Think about your notes...

- Just write on one side of your paper – that will prevent you from turning over or getting lost.
- Don't use paper larger than A5 – the sight of you banging a sheaf of A4 sheets into a neat pile will strike terror into the hearts of your hearers. And anyway, it's much easier to take in a whole sentence (or paragraph) in one glance if the paper is smaller.
- Write the date and the place you gave this talk.
- Store them where they are easy to retrieve.

 What devices do you use to highlight the key words or ideas you want to communicate?

However you do it, make your notes as useful to you – and the people you are speaking to – as possible.

AVOIDING IRRITATING HABITS

We all have our own particular quirks when it comes to speaking in public Some of us fiddle with our wedding rings or keep putting our glasses on and taking them off. Others rock from side to side or run their hands through their hair. It's not that these things are wrong in themselves but, in the end, they can become a fatal distraction.

 What habits should you try to avoid? You may need to consult your best friends.

HUMOURING YOUR HEARERS

Some of the illustrations Jesus uses display a wonderfully rich sense of humour.

 What's good about using humour in sermons?

But be careful. Use humour to underline not to undermine what God wants you to say. The importance of the gospel, the dignity of your ministry as a preacher and, above all, the awesome majesty of God means we can never allow a talk to degenerate into a string of amusing anecdotes.

KEEPING TO TIME

A preacher removing his watch at the start of a sermon once commented, 'My wife tells me this is my most meaningless gesture!' If you are a brilliant speaker or you find yourself in the middle of a revival, you may on occasion trespass on the patience of your hearers. But since few of us are the former and even fewer have experienced the latter, you should aim to keep to the time allotted to you. Make sure you know how long you are being given to speak – and stick to it.

Isn't it unspiritual to be worried about time?

What factors make it important to keep to time? Speaking the truth in love means being concerned not just about the issues we are speaking about but the people to whom we are speaking.

KEEPING UP APPEARANCES

Here are three tips:

- **Be neat and tidy** – your dress sense shouldn't attract attention to you and detract from what you want to say.
- **Stand upright and keep your hands out of your pockets** – putting your hands in your pockets looks untidy and you might find some distracting keys to play with.
- **Use your hands** – well-chosen gestures bring what you are saying to life.

THINK IT THROUGH

*1. Remember, the **way** you say it is as important as **what** you say. Think again about the Feast of Tabernacles in John 7:*

- *How does Jesus use the occasion to engage people's curiosity?*
- *what do the varying reactions tell us about the quality of his communication?*

2. What factors hinder people listening to what you've got to say?

3. What weapons do you have at your disposal to keep people's attention?

FOLLOW IT UP

Prepare a five-minute talk for presentation at a final review session. It can be on any subject you wish.

Continue your studies at home with the

Open Bible Institute
— a thoroughly Bible-centred, distance-learning college

One of the great seats of learning

• **Short Courses in ministry skills:** 10-session courses in Administration, Christian Mission & Ministry, Pastoral Care, Preaching and Youth & Children's Work.

• **The Moore College Correspondence Course:** a great course encompassing biblical studies, church history, doctrine, apologetics and ethics.

• **Certificates of Higher Education:** fully validated qualifications in 'Biblical Studies and Theology' and 'Biblical Studies and Ministry' equivalent to the first year of a degree.

For an information pack or an informal
discussion, please contact:
0845 225 0885
admin@open-bible-institute.org
www.open-bible-institute.org

BE PREPARED
to serve the LORD

***Prepared for Service* provides a unique, part-time training opportunity for both men and women with a desire to serve the Lord Jesus Christ and his people, to be better equipped for works of service in local churches, their communities and the world.**

It aims to achieve this by:

- Offering an environment where gifts and abilities can be realistically assessed to help understand God's purpose for an individual's life

- Providing a biblically-based training resource to help individuals develop knowledge of God's word within the framework of academic study

- Giving practical and pastoral models helping individuals serve in ways that are appropriate to the contemporary world

- Providing teaching, pastoral care and practical experience for individuals with the support of their local churches

For Information Pack/Application Form, please contact:

The 'PfS' Administrators
25, Felton Road,
Poole, Dorset. BH14 0QR

Tel: 01202 738416
Email: pfs@fiec.org.uk
Web: www.fiec.org.uk

A Training Ministry of
The Fellowship of Independent Evangelical Churches

Bible churches together

Could PfS fulfil your needs in serving the LORD?

NOTES

NOTES

NOTES

NOTES

Certification

If you would like your work to be assessed by an independent organisation then please send a clearly named folder containing answers to all the exercises in the this book to the Open Bible Institute:

The Open Bible Institute
Elm House
37 Elm Road
New Malden
Surrey KT3 3HB, UK

A marking fee is payable. For full details please see the website:
www.open-bible-institute.org/learn2lead

Authors

Learn2Lead was developed by:
Brian Boley
Richard Underwood
Paul Mallard
Dr Ray Evans
Tim Saunders